I0224302

# The New Adventures of Jesus:

## Modern Works of Flash Fiction Based on Bible Stories

*by*

# William H. McCann, Jr.

*Finishing Line Press*
Georgetown, Kentucky

# The New Adventures of Jesus:

Modern Works of Flash Fiction Based on Bible Stories

## ACKNOWLEDGMENTS

"On the Road to Damascus" has been previously published in *God Hires Gardeners* (Finishing Line Press, 2023)
"A Visit to Wall Street" was originally accepted for publication in *cc&d magazine* (Scars Publications)

**Disclaimer**:

**This is NOT a work of biblical scholarship.** This is a work of fiction. Names, characters, places, and incidents either are the product of the author's imagination or are used fictitiously and any resemblance to actual persons, living or dead, businesses, companies, events or locales is entirely coincidental.

Publisher: Leah Huete de Maines
Editor: Christen Kincaid
Cover Art: Evan Hammonds
Author Photo: Patrick Mitchell
Cover Design: Zed Saeed


Order online: www.finishinglinepress.com
also available on amazon.com

Author inquiries and mail orders:
Finishing Line Press
PO Box 1626
Georgetown, Kentucky 40324
USA

# Contents

## In the Beginning

I suppose by now that many people know that I died on a cross, spent three days at a wine and cheese party hosted by the Devil, rose from the dead, wandered about saying last goodbyes for 40 days, and finally ascended into heaven. But guess what? As Jack Nicholson once said in *The Shining*, "I'm baaaaaack!"

Jesus Emanuel
Nazareth, Israel

## Jesus and the El Al Captain

Jesus, dressed casually in a pink alligator-adorned golf shirt, khaki pants, and trademarked sandals, was seated in first class on an El Al flight from Israel to Cairo when the plane's captain noticed him. "Umm, aren't you Jesus?"

"I Am. What can I do for you, Captain Morgan?"

"Well, I, uh. How do you know my name?"

"Your name tag?"

"Oh. Yeah," the captain said, still looking at Jesus.

"So, what is your question, sir? "

"Why are you in first class?" blurted the captain.

Jesus just looked up with a perplexed look on his face, so the Captain continued apologetically, "I don't mean to be rude, but don't you still believe that the first shall be last and the last shall be first?"

"I do. But the kind young lady boarding us said that recently the airline president had sent around a memo saying that on each day of Chanukah this year that the last person in line to board is to be upgraded to first class. So here I am. Just as I am."

## Sermon on the Plane

Captain Morgan held the door to the cockpit open, allowing Jesus to enter first; no one was inside. "Are you flying this plane by yourself, Captain?"

"Oh, no. They'll be along." He paused. "May I ask you something. Do you mind?

"Ask away."

"Okay. What do you think are the most important beliefs of Christianity?"

"I dunno," the Lord replied. "I don't know much about Christianity. I'm Jewish. I'm also not much on beliefs. Actions carry more weight."

"Umm, ok," mumbled the captain, a bit dazed and confused.

"Let me put it this way," said Jesus. "My way of looking at things is that everyone should love their God with all their heart and soul, and mind, and their neighbor as much as they love themselves and members of their tribe."

"Isn't that difficult?"

"Of course. Did you think that creating a better world, a peaceful world would be easy?"

"Well, no. But I thought maybe . . . ."

"You thought it was easy just because your friends agree with you? That if people are not—for instance, in the airline industry, then you can make fun of them, bully and revile them, not carry them on your airplane, send them packing, as the Americans might say?"

"Well, I'm not sure I'd confine my 'tribe,' as you say, as narrowly as that, but ... yeah."

"Whom would you exclude?" asked Jesus.

"Just bad people—Palestinians, terrorists, Iranians, you know."

"So like immigrants, people who overstay their visas, lawbreakers, pickpockets, Samarians, prostitutes, and tax collectors?—those last three were big, back in the day, you know."

"Sure. That seems like a pretty good list."

"It does, doesn't it?" said Jesus. "Guess what, Captain Morgan?"

"What?"

"All of those people are your neighbors."

"So what am I to do for my 'neighbors?'" Captain Morgan asked sarcastically.

"Not all that much, really. Just treat them like family, like friends, like... neighbors. It really is that easy, you know."

"Immigrants and terrorists included?"

"Them too," said Jesus.

"Wow. What will my church think if I do that?"

"I think," Jesus said, "that they might think you are a Christian who lives out your beliefs, not just spouts them. But I don't know for sure. I'm Jewish."

3

## A Visit to Wall Street

Jesus was standing in front of the Charging Bull in New York City's famed financial district. After looking at it for a few minutes, he mumbled to himself, "Looks a great deal like Aaron's golden calf grown up and raging down Wall Street."

About that same time a reporter for the *Wall Street Journal* recognized Jesus—who even in the world's financial capital was dressed in khakis, a blue collared golf shirt, and sandals—and asked him a question. "Sir, earlier today there was a near-riot at the Very Very Vinery, Inc. I'd like your thoughts about that."

"About the fact that all of the day laborers, many of them immigrants, hired—some of them only an hour before the close of business—were paid the same daily rate as those hired at 7:30 in the morning who worked from 8 to 6 with two breaks and a meal break?"

"Yes, that's correct. How did you know?"

"There are big screen televisions everywhere in this town, how could I not know?"

"Of course. So what are your thoughts?

"Well, Very, Very, Vinery, Inc. is, what, a $50 billion corporation, right?

"I believe it's at least twice that big, sir."

"Yes. All the better. Under the circumstances, that owner can pay his workers what he wants, when he wants. Simple as that, isn't it? This is America and corporations rule the roost, right?"

"But VVV is not being fair with all of his workers."

"They're not? Each person who was hired was to be paid $100 for the day. Those hired earliest received lunch and two breaks. Those hired later received the same $100 day rate and lunch and breaks as appropriate for the time of day they were hired. From what I can tell, from what reporters have been saying on all those ubiquitous televisions today, the corporation complied with all appropriate wage and hour laws, all requirements for employers whose workers work outside. What's the problem?"

"Those hired last were paid first. That's not right."

"Why not? When you get your paycheck do you know where in line you fell? Was your check written first, last, or someplace in between?"

The reporter stood quiet for a moment so Jesus asked a question. "Is today April First?"

"No, sir. Tuesday, October 29th."

"Ok. A second question, then; is the owner a Christian?"

"I—I don't know. Does that matter?"

"Not to me. But God acts similarly to the way VVV acts. No matter when someone genuinely asks for forgiveness, God gives it. If a person goes to church whenever the door is open, tithes and does everything a Christian is expected to do—wherever they may fall on the gender spectrum—that person will go to heaven. But the same is true of any person who genuinely seeks forgiveness, in their twenties, fifties, nineties or on their deathbed—the same is true. It is equally true of criminals, politicians, even journalists. All of them—the rich and the poor, people of color, and," here Jesus paused for effect, "even you can go to heaven."

"Even me?"

"Even you. Especially you."

And with that Jesus turned and walked down the street and was quickly lost in the rush hour crowd.

## Walking Near Jerusalem

While travelling through Jerusalem, NY to give a speech at a nearby college, Jesus was approached by a young woman and her enthusiastic child. "That's him, Mommy. I know that's him," said the girl.

"Fine," the mother said, irritated. "Are you Jesus?" she practically barked.

"He is, Mommy, he has on his golf shirt with a rainbow on it, khaki pants, and his ubikatis sandals," bubbled the little girl.

"I think she means ubiquitous," said Jesus with a smile. "Sarah is trying to quote from my social media accounts—'Jesus is not who you think you learned about in Sunday School.' Today, only his sandals are ubiquitous. Everything else is new."

"See, Mommy? He even knows my name."

"What can I do for you, Sarah?" asked Jesus.

"My mommy is so lonely. Can you help her be happy, Jesus?"

"What is bothering you, Marisol?" Jesus asked kindly.

"You know my name?" the mother asked, surprised.

"He knows everything, Mommy. He's Jesus Emanuel—God with us."

"Yes, I know your name. Marisol is such a beautiful Spanish name. It translates as 'Mary of Solitude.' And I know that you are lonely, missing your husband who died three years ago." He paused and after a moment he said, "I am sorry."

"Can you bring him back to life for me?" Marisol asked.

"Like you did Lazarus in the Bible?" asked Sarah.

"No. No, I can't do that," said Jesus.

"Tell her she needs to be a wolf," said Sarah

"A wolf?"

"Sarah has been after me to go to college. The local college's teams are nicknamed the Wolves."

"It is a nice place. Walks down by the lake are lovely. Your daughter might be right, Marisol. I do know that you will be fine. Grieving can be a hard thing to get through alone. But you are never alone. Your Father in heaven is always present."

"As close as a prayer," said Sarah.

"Well, I haven't done much praying in the last three years," admitted Marisol.

"You should, Mommy. You should."

Trying to be helpful, Jesus said, "I know that you are an immigrant, that there is much about this country that can be scary and intimidating. But I also know that you're a strong person, Marisol. You speak fluent English. You and your husband made the long and difficult journey to this country. You've got your green card. You'll be okay."

"Oh, Mommy, that's such good news."

"Yes, it is. Or it would be if it were true," said a skeptical Marisol.

"Oh, so the mail hasn't come yet," said Jesus. "It will. And good news with it."

"See, Mommy. See, I told you things would all work out," bubbled Sarah.

"Nothing has worked out—"

"Yet. YET," emphasized Jesus. "Life will always have its troubles and its joys. You've been through a very rough few years, Marisol. But you will smile and laugh again. You'll even have a child again."

"A child? A brother for me?" asked a happy Sarah.

"Perhaps," said Jesus to Sarah before turning to Marisol and adding, "These things take time. It won't happen quickly."

"Yeah," said Sarah. "Nine months."

"Well, a bit longer than that, I'm sure," said her mother with a smile. "I haven't even been on a date since I dated your father. That's been awhile."

"Yes. Well, I'll be speaking down by the lake later this afternoon. Join me if you can."

And they went their separate ways.

**Along the Lake Shore**

After meeting with friends and fans, even a few family members, along the lake shore, Jesus taught them. Hours passed and many realized that they had had nothing to eat. They wondered if anyone had any bread. As they whispered among themselves Jesus said, "Be wary of the bread offered by Democrats and Republicans; be careful, too, of the bread offered by those who are religious."

Puzzled by this remark, they asked each other what Jesus meant by it. Aware of their discussion, Jesus asked, "Are you of so little faith? Why are you talking among yourselves about having no bread? Do you still not understand? How is it you don't understand that I was not talking to you about bread? I am not talking about money, either. Instead, be on your guard against the yeast of those who would seek to influence you."

Then the proverbial lightbulb went on and they understood that he was not telling them to be on guard against the yeast used in bread, but against the teachings of the political and religious leaders who sought to influence them.

## Seeking Jesus

The crowd at the lake was large that afternoon, but two men were there seeking to meet quietly with Jesus for counsel. Seeing a young man named Phillip, a policeman from the local college there to provide crowd control, one of the men told him, "We'd like to invite Jesus to visit our fraternity at Cornell University."

"Are you having a keg party tonight?" asked the policeman.

"Not tonight, sir, we drove here from Cornell," said the second man.

"Very well, follow me, boys," said Phillip as he set off through the crowd searching for Andrew, who was helping organize the day's festivities along the lake shore. Finding Andrew, Phillip told Andrew the mission that the men were on.

Looking at the two men sternly, Andrew said, "Jesus is not available to turn water into beer. If that's what you're about, begone."

"No, sir. We know that," said the first one. "We are seeking after him. Our brothers want him to lead our prayer study later this week."

"Very well, boys," said Andrew, "we'll help you talk to Jesus. Perhaps he will have time to visit Cornell."

Soon the two fraternity brothers, Andrew, and Phillip were able to make their way through the crowd to Jesus. Told of their request, Jesus was willing to visit their fraternity house in coming days.

## The Faith of a Woman from New Canaan, Connecticut

Leaving Jerusalem, Jesus headed toward Tyre, New York when a woman from New Canaan, Connecticut, said, "Lord, Jesus, have mercy on me. My daughter is possessed by TikTok and is suffering terribly."

But Jesus ignored her plea and kept walking. Friends and others who were with him begged Jesus, "Send her away."

Jesus turned to the woman and suggested, "Move to a place where TikTok has been made illegal."

"I can't afford that. Besides, the law may change. Or the lawmakers or the judges may change the law, their minds, or both. But you can help me now."

"It is not for me to interfere in the politics of this place."

"Would you not give me scraps if I were a dog? Is my request any more than table scraps to you? Help my daughter, please."

"Woman, you have great faith. Your request is granted."

And her daughter was healed, never again to be captivated by TikTok.

## Jesus on a Podcast

Jesus was tired, dead tired. He'd been resting quietly for several days at the home of a local rabbi, after having recently walked from Samaria, Michigan to Bethlehem, Pennsylvania. His next trip was to be to Philadelphia—City of Brotherly Love—to speak on a local podcast, "He is With Us."

"Listeners, listen up today," announced Jerry Majors. "Today a man who calls himself 'Jesus' is my guest on WWJD 890 radio on your AM dial. Pick up the phone and call us at 555-555-5666. We want you to have this opportunity to speak with the Lord Jesus Christ. First up is Bob from Bethlehem, P-A. Hi Bob, what's your question for the Lord?"

"Hey, Jesus."

"Hi, Bob, how are you?"

"Good. Very good. Say, I've been wondering, I became a Christian about 6 years ago at the age of 66. Have I really been forgiven for all the things I did wrong before that?"

"Absolutely. Ask and it shall be given unto you. If you sincerely repented of your sins and were baptized, you have been saved. Oh, and I have it on good authority that you did. Congratulations."

"Thank you, Jesus."

"Our next caller today is Adam from New York City," said Jerry.

"Hey, Jerry, many thanks for having Jesus on today's show."

"You're welcome, Adam. What's your question for Jesus?"

"Thank you, Jesus. I just have a quick question for you. Are you a tall white dude like in the picture that hangs in my church? A dude with a brown beard, white skin, and flowing white robes that seem to attract children like sugar water does hummingbirds?"

"Well, Adam, I don't want to disappoint you, but I'm not a Christian at all. I was raised a Jew. My parents and I were immigrants on the run for several years before we could get back to Bethlehem—the original one in Israel, not the one just down the road from Philly, here.

"And, oh, yeah, I'm a person of color. My skin tone is closer to that of Martin Luther King, Jr. than that of either John or Bobby Kennedy."

"Thank you for your question, Adam," said Jerry, the show's host.

Moments later, Jerry said, "Jesus, I think you probably surprised that caller with your answer. But tell me, do you know those three gentlemen?"

"Oh, absolutely. And Abraham Lincoln, too."

"And that's our cue to go to a commercial. So here's a little bit of Marvin Gaye singing 'Abraham, Martin, and John' to take us into that break." As the music swelled, Jerry said, "We're out. We have 90 seconds to chew the fat a bit. Hearing our caller's gasps when you said you were a person of color may have elicited a louder gasp than when you admitted to being Jewish. What'd you think?"

"I am who I yam."

"That you are. Say, do you know Popeye, too?"

"Oh, no. He's just a cartoon character," said Jesus.

"I know. I just thought that maybe you'd made him into a real man. Just like Pinocchio was made into a real boy."

"No. I'm afraid you're confusing me with Walt Disney."

## Jesus Takes a Walk

After nearly an hour of answering questions, some of which were clearly angering Jerry Majors' listeners, one of the host's minions texted the host. "All hell has broken loose. Check it out on WNBC!"

Majors turned on the TV sitting on his desk to see that his assistant was right. The local news station had a camera crew and reporter stationed outside the building where the podcast was being broadcast, covering the angry mob that had gathered to protest Jesus' being on the podcast.

"Oh, my," said Jesus when shown the video. "I guess we're done here, aren't we?"

"Yes. At least for today," said the radio and podcast host. "But I do hope you'll come back soon—this'll be great for ratings."

"No doubt," said Jesus before he walked through the locked fire escape door and down those steps towards safety. Nearing the bottom of the stairs and noticing some of the protesters angrily running towards him, Jesus simply walked on air across to another building, where he walked through its exterior wall and into the unisex bathroom behind it. Then he washed his hands, opened the door and walked to the elevator. Soon enough he was safely on the ground floor, where the concierge hailed him a cab.

## Whose God?

Jesus, dressed in khakis, a collared golf shirt, and sandals, came upon an argument between a Christian and a Jew. Each man was absolutely certain that theirs was the 'only true religion.' Seeing Jesus, each man was certain that Jesus would take his side; so almost in unison the men said, "Whose God is the true God and whose is a fake?"

Jesus replied, "There is only one God. He simply has more than one name. And there are many ways to worship."

"So," the Sunday School teacher asked, "God is a benevolent white guy with a long white beard that trails to the ground?"

"I think," Jesus responded, "that when you finally meet God that you will be astounded at them."

"So God is non-binary?"

"I think," Jesus repeated, "that when you meet God, you will be astounded."

## Who Created Ants and Giraffes?

A young evangelical lawyer, fresh from having passed the bar exam to become a practicing attorney, confronted Jesus, "What does the Bible say about gay people?"

"I don't know," Jesus said. "I'm a Jew, not a Christian. What do you say that it says?"

"It says in Leviticus 18:22 that a man lying with a man is an abomination before God."

"Ok." Jesus paused. "Well, who wrote the Bible?"

"God."

"Really? I thought that your Christian Bible said that God actually only wrote what are called the 10 Commandments on tablets made of stone."

"Well, literally speaking, you're correct. But the Bible is the inerrant word of God."

"Ok," Jesus said. "Let's, for the sake of argument, assume that the Bible is infallibly correct, despite the fact that God only wrote the 10 Commandments. What human being do you know who never makes a mistake?"

"No one. I don't know a perfect person. No one, history teaches, is infallible—except you, of course," conceded the lawyer, nervous about where this might be headed.

Changing the topic, Jesus asked, "Who created ants, or for that matter alligators, giraffes, children, and mountains and rivers, the Earth and all that is on or in it?"

"God," quickly answered the puzzled inquisitor.

"And God, wouldn't you agree, as the children's Sunday School song says, loves all children 'red and yellow, black and white, all are precious in his sight, all the children of the world?'" asked Jesus.

"Actually, the song says, Jesus Loves the Little Children," corrected the lawyer.

"You're right, of course. So you think that God doesn't love the little children?"

"No. No. I didn't say that. Of course God loves all the little children. After all, he's your father, right?"

"Right." Jesus paused. "So," he asked, "why wouldn't God love all the children of the world when they grow up? Black and white, red and yellow, differently abled, smart and not so smart, gay and transgendered, God created them all, as you said earlier. Why wouldn't he love them all as adults? Why would any of them be viewed as unlovable? Aren't all persons worthy of the same kindnesses due every other person on planet Earth? After all, didn't God create them all?"

"You just don't understand," muttered the lawyer as he turned and walked away.

## Jesus Visits Nebo, Kentucky

Jesus was in Nebo, in Hopkins County, to attend dirt car races at a nearby track. The next day, after couch surfing at a friend's house, he went to church with his friend's family. The church's pastor greeted Jesus with great enthusiasm despite the fact that Jesus was wearing khaki shorts, a golf shirt, and sandals; hardly suitable attire for church, he thought. Still, after introducing Jesus to the congregation the pastor asked, "Jesus, would you like to read from the Bible for us this morning? Perhaps sing us a song?"

So Jesus rose from his seat, went forward and read.

But as he read, a murmur arose among those who were listening. "Isn't he from Nazareth?" "Near Bardstown? I don't think so. Some place further east, I think." "Do you suppose he might be able to turn my water into bourbon?" "What is he doing here?" "Doesn't he know that Brother Jones is better at reading scripture than this racing fan? I, too, like dirt racing, but that doesn't make me able to speak even well-known biblical truths."

After the service Jesus was ignored and all went and gathered around their pastor and praised him.

Jesus and those with him simply left and started walking towards Madisonville.

## Let Go and Let God

Jesus was fishing on Herrington Lake with a few friends when one asked him, "Rabbi, who is my neighbor? I understand that I am to love the Lord God, and my neighbor as myself, but in this social media age where it is possible to know of natural disasters and murders and mass shootings as they are happening 24/7/365, I need a little clarity."

"Well, John Paul, I recommend what a wise woman once told a friend of mine: 'Trust God to take care of what you cannot.' You are human, with family, friends, jobs, and obligations. It is not possible to be concerned with everyone, with all of the world's problems. Sometimes you may be able to provide a donation of a few dollars, perhaps even a few hundred dollars. But no one person can do it all. Still, you can pray that those affected receive the help they need from those who have the time or money or both to help. And you can, as the old saying goes, 'Let go and let God.' To do that is not to ignore your obligations to help your neighbor; rather it is a recognition that you, as a single person, cannot help all of your neighbors all of the time."

## Goth Girl at the Well

Jesus was seated next to a "wishing well" in a mall not far from Samaria, Indiana when a teenage goth girl, dark makeup, rings in her nose and ears, maybe 16 or 17, approached him.

"Give me water," the Lord said.

"Mister, that's not a real well. It's an ad for the Dream Well. If you're in need of help or are ill, you write your wish on a piece of paper and drop it in the well bucket. If you pray, or believe in Santa Claus, or whatever, your wish may be granted."

"Give me water."

"Didn't you understand me? It's not a real well. But you can buy water at several places in the mall."

"I know," said Jesus. "But if water comes out, wouldn't you agree that it's a real well?"

"Well, doh," the girl said. "But this one is made of cardboard. Look, I can pick it up. See?"

"Yes, I see. You've shown it to the mall walkers and other people, too. Now, set it back down, take the bucket, empty it of paper wishes, and dip it in the well."

By now the little scene at the wishing well had gained a little notice. As Goth Girl emptied the bucket, its wishes fluttered to the floor, causing at least a couple of people to slow their rush through the mall to see what was going on at the display.

"It's not a real well. But, oh, gawd, wait here and I'll get you some water. I'll be right back."

"No. Don't do that. Just dip the bucket into the well," said Jesus.

"Oh, alright. I'll humor you."

And then the Goth Girl from Samaria, Indiana tossed the bucket into the well, then turned the wooden handle to raise the bucket. But as she did so, water sloshed out of the bucket onto the mall floor and onto her and Jesus. "Oh, I'm sorry," she said. "Did I get you wet, too?"

"No. No, I'm fine," replied Jesus with a small smile. Some of the mall walkers having seen what happened started to clap. Jesus shushed them with a look.

"I . . . I didn't mean to get you wet. How did that happen? Where did that water come from?

"Me. I did that. I am the source of living water. She who believes in me will never thirst."

"What, you invent an app or something?"

"No. I am. I am the source of living water. I am the way to heaven."

"Ok," Goth Girl said, "I have to go. You sell your 'Living Water' to these nice folks who have gathered around. Mom's expecting me home for dinner."

And Goth Girl left.

But several who had witnessed what happened, stayed and talked with Jesus and he convinced many.

## Questions

While attending an arts festival in Mt. Angel, Oregon, Jesus was approached by a Benedictine monk from the nearby abbey. As Jesus spoke, surrounded by a large crowd, the monk stood and listened to the answers being given to the inquisitive crowd.

"Do you believe in the death penalty, Jesus?" someone asked.

"Now, what do you think," Jesus answered impishly, a twinkle in his eyes. An appreciative chuckle went through the crowd.

"I know," the woman continued, "that you were wrongly crucified, I get that. But my sister was raped, tortured, and finally murdered. Doesn't she deserve justice? Doesn't the man who was convicted of that murder deserve to die for his crime?"

"Brenda," Jesus said, addressing the woman directly, "your sister does deserve justice. But Sally will not get justice if the state of Idaho of kills the innocent man convicted of her horrible death."

"OMG," the surprised Brenda exclaimed. "Can't you do something?" she asked.

"Pray. And always keep in mind that justice is the province of God, and not of men and women. Only God can always be certain of what is right and true, of where true justice lies."

## Jesus Punks an Atheist

In a Minneapolis park on a chilly fall night, Jesus and some believers were seated around a small fire, burning marshmallows and sharing s'mores, when he was approached by a man who introduced himself by saying, "Are you Jesus?"

"I am."

"Are you God?"

"I am."

"Are you the Holy Spirit?

"I am."

"I don't believe. I am an atheist."

But even before the word "atheist" was fully out of the man's mouth Jesus was gone. Nothing was left. Only Jesus' stick was on the ground, its marshmallow lying amidst ashes.

It took a few moments—it was dark, except in the immediacy of the flames—for those sitting around the fire that night to realize that Jesus was gone. He had simply vanished. Disappeared.

"Jesus?" the atheist asked. "Where are you?"

Some of the believers, realizing suddenly that Jesus was gone turned accusingly toward the atheist and asked, "What did you do? Who are you to send Jesus away?"

But before the atheist could answer them, or before the crowd could harm him, Jesus appeared again where he'd been sitting, the ash-covered marshmallow and stick in his hand.

"Were you looking for me?" asked Jesus of the atheist.

"I was."

"Then are you truly an atheist?"

## An Atheist has Questions for Jesus

Ignoring Jesus' question of him, the atheist asked, "How is it possible that you can be God, Jesus, and Holy Ghost?"

"Why," Jesus said, "I can be that in the same way, Saul, that you can be Dad or Father to your son, Honey to your wife, and Mr. Good to your employees. We all have different ways that others see us, different ways in which those other people empower us, or we empower them."

"Oh," Saul Good responded.

"Would you like to join us?" asked Jesus.

"May I? I do have some more questions," responded Saul.

"Mr. Good," said a voice from nearby, "would you like to roast some marshmallows, perhaps enjoy some S'mores with us? Many of us have questions too, even those of us who believe."

So Saul Good joined the group and asked many questions before later going on his way.

## Mary Confronts Jesus

She was angry—seething. When she saw Jesus sitting at the drug store's fountain in the mall—a milkshake in front of him—she ran towards him demanding, "Why did you bother my little girl? I'm sure she meant you no harm!" Goth Girl's mother spewed.

"Who are you?" Jesus asked, no anger of any kind present in his gentle voice.

"I'm Martha's mother. At 16 she thinks she's a grown woman. But you scared her enough that she came home for dinner tonight."

"That is unusual," remarked Jesus in a tone that did not allow listeners to fully understand what he meant.

"It is only Martha and me. What did you do?"

"I offered her Living Water."

"Living Water?"

"She can drink and never again be thirsty."

"Drink and never be thirsty?"

"Do you not hear? Yes, I can give her, or you, Living Water that will keep you from ever again being thirsty."

"And why would you do that?" asked Mary.

"I asked Martha for a sip of water. She said there was none in the well I was sitting beside. Then she offered to go get me some water from a restaurant. Before she left I asked her to dip water out of the well beside me."

"But that well is made of cardboard."

"So Martha said, too. And she was about to leave when I asked her to dip water from the well. Then she did dip her bucket into the well and brought up water—Living Water, I called it. Martha immediately headed home. Now," Jesus asked, "may I give you some Living Water?"

"Life is hard. I have no time for fantasy and fictions of this sort. Living Water, indeed," muttered Mary, starting to leave.

"So, Mary, are you going home to bring your husband back to speak with me?"

"I have no husband. I am simply going home, leaving you to your silliness."

"You speak the truth, Mary. You have had four husbands but you are not married now."

"How do you know that?" an astonished Mary asked. "Are you a prophet?"

"No," he paused. "No, Mary, I'm no prophet. But I do know that you live with Ringo—he who is neither a Starr, nor a drummer. Would you like some Living Water? Would you like to never again be thirsty?"

"Well," Mary slowly said, gathering her thoughts. "I have some questions first."

And so Mary stayed and spoke with Jesus and others who were there. Eventually, a mall security guard came up and spoke to the group. "I'm sorry," she said. "But it is time for the mall to close. If you are a walker you may come back at 7 in the morning; if you want to shop, stores begin opening at 9 am. Please come back tomorrow."

So they left together, walking down the street to an all-night diner called the Night Hawk, where the conversation continued for hours more. Eventually, Mary invited Jesus to come home and stay with she and Martha and Ringo—he who was not a drummer, but a paralegal—to spend a few days.

## Jesus and the Cross

Jesus, dressed in a coat and tie and his ubiquitous sandals, was standing backstage at The Lord of Host's Ministries as senior minster Rob Maloney was taking the show to break.

"Friends," Dr. Maloney said, "in a moment we'll be back and I'll speak with Jesus Christ, himself. Indeed, I met the true Lord of Hosts on an El Al flight recently while flying home from a trip to the Holy Land. Stay tuned."

"Annnd, we're out," said the stage manager. "Sixty seconds of commercials."

"Thank you, sixty-seconds," said Dr. Maloney as he crossed to Jesus.

"Impressive program today," said Jesus with a smile.

"All due to you, sir."

"Just call me Jesus. Or you might call me what some do when they strike their finger with a hammer, 'Jesus H. Christ.'"

"I think I'll stick with just Jesus," said the evangelist with his own smile.

"Back in 15," said the stage manager.

"Thank you, fifteen," said Dr. Maloney as he started to cross back to his spot on the stage.

A crew member appeared at Jesus' side. "When we come back, Doc will give a brief promo and then introduce you." After a pause she asked, "Are you really *the* Jesus?"

"I am."

"Back in three, two, one," said the stage manager.

"Alright, we're back," said Dr. Maloney. "But before I introduce our guest, let me ask you to support this important ministry in any amount. Whether you have a widow's mite of just a few pennies or a hundred dollars, your donation is what helps keep us on the air. But if you have a bit more you might want to become a Disciple for a monthly donation of $20; we here at Lord of Hosts Ministries will send you this beautiful olive tree wood cross. Or, for $99 monthly you can become a Lord's Apostle and I will send you a cross immersed in the urine of the Lord of Hosts him—"

And just at that moment Jesus went barreling out of the wings and did a flying tackle of Dr. Maloney as crew members flew onto the stage and the director took the show to an unplanned commercial break.

## Police Question Jesus

When things had been calmed down, order restored, and police arrived to take over from show security personnel, the police had some questions for Jesus.

"What is your name, sir?" asked one of the policemen who had been dispatched to the scene.

"Jesus."

"Just Jesus?"

"If Pink and Lizzo and Elvis can go by single names, I can, too."

"I suppose," said the cop somewhat skeptically. "But for the record?"

"For the record it is Jesus Emanuel."

"Jesus Emanuel," the policeman repeated back.

"God With Us."

"Of course. So what happened?"

"So, Dr. Maloney—who claims to be a man of God—apparently invaded my privacy and took some urine out of the restroom in my dressing room and was in the process of selling it on TV! I guess I kind of lost it and took him down."

"I'd say," murmured the cop. "So that was why you tackled the guy? Personal hurt?"

"That, and that he was committing fraud, since I knew he and his people had not come into the dressing room. At least Mapplethorpe used his own pee when he put a cross in a bottle of it. Besides, I haven't peed in like 2000 years, so it's not possible for him to have any of my urine to sell."

"2000 years?"

"Something like that."

"Um, you look like you might be mid-thirties."

"Yeah, well, crucifixion stops the aging process."

"Oh. Yeah, of course it does. Have you ever done this kind of thing before?"

"Just once. I ran the money changers out of the temple many years ago in my hometown, or maybe it was another town. I'm afraid my memory isn't what it used to be."

As Jesus finished talking, a second policeman—a young woman, actually—entered the room. "Do we want to take him in for further questioning, Sandy?" she asked.

"Does Dr. Maloney want to press charges, Jean?"

"No. He and his team are trying to figure out what to tell their studio audience, how to address questions that the press will have. Important stuff."

"Is the good doctor okay?" asked Jesus.

"Oh, he's fine. Just worried about his bank balances," said Jean.

"Well, I guess you're free to go, then," said Sandy.

And with that Jesus turned and walked out through the wall. Once out on the street Jesus hailed a cab and headed back to his hotel. It had been a long day.

## Reason for the Season

Jesus was visiting a shopping mall in suburban Salt Lake City when a little girl, four, maybe five, approached Jesus and said, "I just saw Santa Claus."

"Oh," said Jesus.

"That's right," said the girl's father. "Santa Land is just past the jewelry store on the right."

"Yes, I stopped there earlier."

"You did?" said the girl. "What did you tell Santa that you wanted for Christmas?"

"Well, Dottie," said the father, "I doubt that Jesus asked for anything."

"But why not?" she asked her father. "Haven't you been good this year?" she asked Jesus.

"Well, dear, Jesus—"

"Jesus? Are you *the* Jesus? Like the man in the Bible?" asked Dottie.

"No. This man isn't Jesus," said her father. "He doesn't look anything like the Jesus at church. Besides that, Jesus lived 2,000 years ago. This man looks to be only about 30 years old."

"Well, I am Jesus. I came back to see what has been going on since I last walked the earth."

"I don't believe you," said the father.

"Alright, Thomas, feel my hands."

"How'd he know your name, Daddy?" asked Dottie.

Holding out his hands, Jesus asked Thomas, "Can you feel the places in my palms where the nails held me to the cross?" Putting a foot up on a nearby chair, Jesus asked, "Dot, can you see a scar on my ankle where the nail was pounded through to hold my feet?"

"Daddy, there is a big dent in his ankle," said Dottie. Looking up at Jesus she asked, "Do your ankles hurt?"

"Not now, Dear. But they once did."

"Are you really Jesus," asked Thomas, the father of Dottie. "You don't look like what I've been told all my life what Jesus looked like. How can you be Jesus?"

"I am who I've always been," said Jesus. "But more than 2,000 years ago there were no cameras, no cellphones either—so no photographs."

"So you're really Jesus?"

"I am, Thomas."

"Well, it's a little hard to comprehend. But I've seen the nail holes, put my fingers in the scars. I believe you are who you say you are."

"Who is he, Daddy?"

"This is Jesus. Dottie, Jesus is the reason for the season."

"So you bring presents to good boys and girls?"

"Sort of," said Jesus. "But my presents are not for every good boy and girl.

Only girls and boys who believe in me get can have eternal life."

"Can I see you again next Christmas? Will I see you at church or school?" asked Dottie.

"Maybe sometime," said Jesus, who then disappeared.

"Where did Jesus go?" asked Dottie.

A confused Thomas, father of Dottie, said, "I, I don't know. I guess it's time to go home."

Moments later as they approached a mall door leading outside, Dottie pulled away from her father and ran toward Jesus. "You are Jesus. You are. Daddy, Jesus is back!"

"Yes, he is," said her father.

"Will you stay around from now on, Jesus?" asked the little girl.

"I am always here. I am always as close as a prayer, as easily seen as a butterfly," said Jesus. "I won't always be where you can see me. But I can always hear your prayers. Just say your prayers and I will be listening, Dot," said Jesus.

"Did you hear that, Daddy? Jesus called me Dot."

"I did," said Jesus.

"Come on, Dottie," said her father.

"Call me Dot, Dad. If Jesus is going to call me Dot, you and Mom should, too."

## Jesus and the Athlete

Walking through a park on the outskirts of Atlanta, Jesus stopped to watch a one-on-one basketball game.

With a final long fadeaway jumper the taller, more athletic teen declared, "That's 30, and three in a row. See you later, Lenny Loser." And he walked away.

Lenny, for that was his name, looked devastated and frustrated, so Jesus walked up to him.

"Tough loss, huh?"

"Yeah. Real tough. That last game I lost by only a basket. I thought maybe God would help me win it."

"Oh," Jesus said, "why would he do that?"

"I'm Christian."

"That's it? That guy outweighs you, is taller than you, and is a better shot from behind the arc. Heck, he even let you count threes that were shorter than his."

"But he's not a Christian."

"How do you know he's not?" asked a puzzled Jesus.

"He doesn't go to church."

"Do you have to go to church to be a Christian?"

"Probably not. I skip church sometimes, when I'm sick," added Lenny.

"Or when you don't want to go," added Jesus.

"Ok. That's true, too." Lenny stopped and looked into Jesus' eyes. "How'd you know?"

"I was a child once, too, Lenny."

"Yeah. Sure."

"Say," asked Jesus, "you wanna play a game or two?"

And so they did.

## Questions in Mt. Angel

At a custom car show in Mt. Angel, Oregon, Jesus found himself surrounded by men and women seeking answers to their questions. One woman spoke from near the back of the crowd to ask, "Do you believe in the death penalty?"

"No," responded Jesus. "Why do you believe in it, Brenda?"

Brenda, for that was indeed her name, said, "Sir, my sister was murdered and her killer has been convicted in a court of law in another state. Soon he will face his maker if I have anything to do with it. I want justice for my sister."

"And how," Jesus asked, "will the killing of an innocent man serve justice for your sister Sally?"

Brenda, shocked, asked, "You mean he didn't do it?"

"He didn't do it. The man is guilty of many things—being poor, being a Mexican immigrant, not speaking fluent English, being willing to say anything in order to get some sleep after fourteen hours of interrogation. But he's innocent of killing your sister. The police need to focus their investigation on people who speak fluent English and have the same skin color as your mother."

"My mother? OMG, I need to go." And she left quickly to see if she could do anything to help find her sister's real killer.

"Jesus, I have a question," said a Benedictine monk from the nearby abbey, in town to run an errand for the abbot. "Do you believe in abortion?"

"No." Jesus paused then continued. "Yet, there are clearly instances where an abortion is the correct medical decision. And there may be other instances where that is the correct ethical or moral decision. Which is why I think that the decision is one best made after consultations with God through prayer, or for a woman and her family to make with their doctor and their God."

"So there are no consequences for having an abortion?"

"Yes," Jesus said, "of course there are consequences. Some will be suffered in this world. And other consequences will be meted out by God. Some of those consequences will be for having had an abortion, others will be for having prohibited an abortion. Indeed, everyone will be judged by God. And ultimately that is the only consequence that matters. To deprive someone of communion or burial in holy ground are of no consequence to God, and such actions mean nothing to me. The length of history is long and God will judge every person in His time, not yours."

The monk hurried back to the Abbey, his errand in town forgotten.

## Jesus Holds a Press Conference

A few days after he ever-so-briefly appeared on Dr. Maloney's television show, Jesus was approached about having a press conference. It was not something he wanted to do, but 'friends' prevailed upon him, reminding him that his popularity had plunged recently. "Your Q-rating is in the toilet," one friend said.

"What's a Q-rating?"

"It means, Jesus, that your message is not being heard because a lot of people think you're just a bully who attacked that nice Dr. Maloney."

"Yeah, well, he was cheating people—or at least trying to."

"I understand," said the publicist. "But a lot of people don't."

"Oh, alright," mumbled a still-reluctant Lord of Hosts.

Hours later the publicist had called in some favors and gathered a few media types for a Q&A with Jesus. "Thank you all for coming. We welcome our friends from local news outlets, CNN, CBN, and CBS as well as the Christian Science Monitor and People Magazine. We do appreciate your time. Without further ado let me introduce Jesus Emmanuel."

"Jesus, Jesus, Jesus!" His name rang out numerous times and not a single knee bowed. Instead, Jesus simply said, "I am."

Someone from *People Magazine* asked, "If your name is Jesus Emmanuel, who is Jesus Christ?"

"Oh, that's me. Just like your name your nom de plume is Andrea French, but your real name is Angela Joyce—Jesus Emmanuel, which means God With Us, is my real name, even though many know me as Jesus Christ."

Seeing shocked looks on several faces, Jesus said, "I do apologize, Angie."

"Um, sure. Can I ask a follow-up question?"

"Sure."

"Who do you support for president?"

"I don't vote."

"So you're not a patriotic American?" asked a Christian Broadcast Network reporter.

"Of course not. I'm an immigrant. I'm homeless, and I'm not an American." Jesus paused. "Next question?"

"Sir, will you support efforts to make this a Christian nation?"

"I'm Jewish."

"Are you dead?"

"I am."

"But you're standing here before us."

"So you say."

And with that Jesus ascended back into the heavens. And the camera people kept their lenses focused on Him until He was hidden by the clouds.

Guess what story led news broadcasts that evening?

The next day, a Sunday, found no more people in churches across the country than had been there the week before. And by Tuesday morning the *Today Show* had two experts on to explain the magic trick that allowed Jesus to ascend into heaven without any obvious wires or propulsion devices.

# What's Love Got to Do With It?

Jesus' long trip to Emmaus, Texas was nearly at an end when his American Airlines flight landed at Love Field, near Dallas, Texas. Twenty minutes or so later, after renting a car, Jesus headed towards I-20 and what he figured to be a two-hour trip, what with his tendency to get lost in big city traffic—any town with more than one stoplight.

About the time Jesus was disembarking his flight, two Dallas area theologians were heading towards a church conference at Emmaus, about 135 miles from Dallas on I-20 E. About an hour into the two hour trip the car engine started to cough and sputter; eventually, it died. An examination of the engine gave them no clues as to what might be wrong. One of the two had left his cell phone on his office desk. The other's phone battery died simultaneously with their car. They were stranded! No way to call anyone for help.

Ten or 15 minutes later Jesus, wearing his usual golf shirt, khaki shorts, and sandals drove up and asked the ministers if he could help them. "Well, we are in a bit of a hurry. John's phone is on his desk, my battery is dead."

"I don't know what we do now," said John. "We are to speak at a Christian conference in Emmaus later this afternoon."

"I'm headed toward Emmaus, too. Would you like a ride?"

"Umm. Okay. That'd be very nice," said Rob.

"What about your car?" asked Jesus.

"It's a rental," said John. "I'll call the agency from the conference. I'm pretty sure they'll bring us a replacement vehicle for the drive back to Dallas on Sunday morning."

"Well, okay then. Let me help you transfer your stuff to the trunk of my car," said Jesus.

When they were on the road a few minutes later, Jesus asked, "What's the topic of the conference, a Christian conference, I think you called it?"

"Love is the general topic," said John.

"I tend to think of the conference as being about WWJL—Who Would Jesus Love?" said Rob. "

And who do you think that Jesus wouldn't love?" asked Jesus, realizing that he had not been recognized.

"Well," Rob replied, "I don't think there is anyone who Jesus didn't love, that were he here today, that he wouldn't love."

"That's true," said John. "Though I do think that there are sins he didn't approve of."

"So you're saying that Jesus would love the sinner and hate the sin?" Jesus asked.

"Exactly!" both men chorused.

"So how do you think you might love the sinner if you hate what they do? Is that even possible?"

"I do think it is difficult," said Rob. "But as Christians we're asked to do just that."

"Well," Jesus asked, "there are a lot of Christians today who serve in legislatures, on school boards and in Congress, as well as elsewhere in public life. Right?"

"True," both ministers concurred.

"I worked back in the 1980s to help create a Moral Majority in this country," said John.

"And I have supported Christians running for public office, too," said Rob.

"So you supported Donald Trump?"

"Oh, of course," said John and Rob almost in chorus.

"Didn't you?" asked Rob.

"No, I'm not registered to vote in Texas," answered Jesus, deflecting the question a bit. "But tell me, in what ways is Donald Trump a Christian? He wants to send immigrants packing when your Bible speaks about welcoming the stranger. He wants to reduce food aid to poor people when in ancient times, societies allowed the poor and the hungry to glean the wheat left along the edges of the fields, so that they might have something to eat. He seems to lack empathy for anyone but himself, and perhaps a few family members. I'm Jewish, I'm not a Christian. But aren't things like compassion for the poor, the hungry, the homeless and the immigrant basic beliefs of Christians?"

The question was left hanging as Jesus pulled into the venue for the Christian conference in Emmaus. "I think we're here, gentlemen. May I help you unload the trunk and carry things inside?"

Both Rob and John were a bit surprised. But looking around they saw the sign: "Welcome to Emmaus' Love for All Conference June 6-9 Preaching, Teaching, and Reaching Out in Love to the World. Join us! No Admission. Great Preaching. Wonderful Music! And the Word of God With Us Daily."

"Well, I guess we are. Thank you for the ride and the conversation, Friend," said Rob.

"Would you care to join us for the conference?" asked John.

"No, I can't do that. But I do appreciate the offer."

"Well, can you please tell us your name. We'd certainly like to thank you for your generosity today."

"Better yet," said Jesus, "here's my card."

The card read 'Jesus Emmanuel. God with US. Reachable by prayer 24/7/365.'

When the two men looked up from the card seconds later, Jesus and his car were gone. And the men's luggage was nearby.

## On the Road to Damascus

Driving towards Damascus, VA after a long day, it was almost inevitable that Kevin would pull over for a brief nap. He had gone through he didn't know how many small towns, wanting to stop for a cup of caffeine—it didn't matter if it was tea, or coffee, or an energy drink. But at every opportunity he'd not bought anything. This damn Covid-19 pandemic might mean he wouldn't be able to find a place to pee later. Besides, the Lord would keep him alert.

So he held his eyelids open with toothpicks and drove on.

Approaching Damascus Kevin found a wide spot in the road and pulled over. Kla-thump. Kla-thump. As he settled in for "ten," he thought that before he went on, he'd better check out his tires; he might have a flat. Maybe two. But first he wanted a bit of shut eye.

Kevin was uncertain how long he'd been asleep. It might have been minutes. It might have been hours. Suddenly he was awakened by the long lonesome sounds of a train whistle—literally right beside him. The train's lights filled his car. But even before he could move his car off the tracks, or even could turn its engine on—the train was crushing his car, and his spirit was travelling upwards.

"Kevin," chided Jesus, "I kept suggesting the caffeine drinks."

"That was you? I thought it was Satan, trying to play a joke on me."

"Nope."

Kevin responded without thinking. "Oh, well, live and learn, I guess,"

"Except you did neither."

"Ya got me there, Jesus."

"No. I've got you here. Welcome to heaven, Kevin."